Ifs, Ifs, Ifs

musings by
David G. Walker

Červená Barva Press
P.O. Box 440357
W. Somerville, MA 02144-3222

www.cervenabarvapress.com

Bookstore: www.thelostbookshelf.com

Cover art: "Three Little Pigs - the wolf lands in the cooking pot" Leonard Leslie Brooke (1862-1940)

Cover design: William J. Kelle

ISBN: 978-1-950063-49-9

ACKNOWLEDGEMENTS

The following poem has appeared in the following magazine: "If, After Reading Emerson's Nature, I Have a Transparent Eyeball Experience and a Pen Handy" in *The Kitchen Poet,* "If We Were Connected" in *Menacing Hedge,* and "If You Leave the Radio On" in *Philosophical Idiot.* David would also like to thank his family, friends, and mentors for always supporting his efforts, creative or otherwise, without whose guidance he would surely be lost within the thickets of his own mind and love for caffeinated beverages.

TABLE OF CONTENTS

For you, holding this book – especially if your name is Caitlin

Ifs, Ifs, Ifs

If, After Reading Emerson's *Nature*, I Have a Transparent Eyeball Experience and a Pen Handy

I do not need my lungs.
I adapt and learn to live without,
no longer dependent on air
to get that hammer inside my chest
swinging –
feeling more alive than ever.

I become aware that I do not see
but rather occupy
a cranium-sized room with the shades
pulled open.

I am permeable.
I reach higher and lower states
of consciousness between each street light
I pass without feeling pride
or guilt.

I don't blink to moisturize my eyes;
I do it for the experience of seeing
the world afresh a thousand times an hour.

Calculations to cure cancer are
written on each signal sent to
wiggle my toes.

I feel the water in my body tugging
towards the faucets.
I become liquid.
Drink me down.

We are part and parcel of one another
now.
We always have been.

Now aim me, hours later,
on your favorite tree or pages
of a book written in braille
because you never learned to digest
with anything other than your
eyes.

I want you to transmogrify,
like me,
down the drain,
be flushed and follow pipes
to dreams you didn't even know
you had.

Wake up with the shades drawn,
that hammer swinging
Thumps into your chest.

Drop your lungs off next
to your keys and inhale deeply.

If Santa Offed Himself

I have the original Dead Santa Ornament. I can still smell the formaldehyde. One day, when Santa was knocking a few back with Rudolf – of course Rudolf lapping his bourbon from a trough – he decided that enough was enough. Enough listening to kids screaming up at him from his lap demanding electronics that cost more than the yearly salary of a high school teacher in America. Enough of the missus complaining, who couldn't understand how one night demanded so much preparation that he couldn't give *her* one night of meaningful conversation. Enough of the endless hounding of his nutritionist who kept lecturing, "Just because it's there doesn't mean you have to eat it." So he hung himself with Christmas lights. Dangling, he was found, preserved, and given to elves who know only how to hammer, painted after posed to sparkle in the glittering lights of sugar cookies and crayon wishes.

Now, in a few years, he will catch a pretty penny on Ebay when a bidding war ensues until Sportfan2012 finally caves and goes to the Buy It Now price. That pretty penny will blossom into a small fortune if I hold on to it longer. My granddaughter will be sitting at an odd angle from a white haired man with a bowtie and a beige sweater vest – if such fashions are still reserved for the pompous hosts of *Antiques Roadshow* at the time. He will point to the Santa hat, mildewed despite the preservation chemicals, the oddly ragged indent where reds and greens dug into his neck, the loss of value due to a set of replacement lights. *All in all, not a bad piece.*

If This Title Does Not Contextualize

Let me set the scene for you:

A man and woman are walking down the street
of an eerily empty city sidewalk. The man has the hand
of their daughter's in his. She has a balloon in
her other hand. The balloon is red.

Now I will describe a seemingly obscure and meaningless
event and give it some obscure and meaningless meaning.

The daughter was vigilant in watching her feet,
careful not to endanger her mother. The wind picks
up and blows the balloon, violently twisting
the string until the daughter is forced to let it go.
As she watches the balloon become engulfed
by the clouds high above her head, she can feel the terrain
under her feet change. She stops and looks down
in horror. A crack rests below her sole and looks like a
perfect bisection of her foot. She can almost imagine
her foot in two pieces, but this is nothing compared
to the fate that awaits her mother.

At this point, I have lost the audience. They are not
invested in the plot nor the characters I have inadequately
introduced. I am not unaware of this fact, so I throw a
Hail Mary and forward the plot in an absurd and
unrealistic way.

She begins to cry violently. Her father bends
down to remedy the situation. He begins to wipe
her tears away and speak soothingly though the cause
of her distress is unknown to him. The mother
walks towards the street to hail a cab. Her heel
gets caught in a deep crack and snaps off, causing
her to lose her balance. She falls towards the street just

as a cab is passing. She twists in an attempt to avoid the blow but is only somewhat successful. She fractures several bones in her back.

After this pathetic excuse for wit, I will try to universalize the message with a completely random and ineffective metaphor.

As her mother was being loaded into the ambulance, she couldn't help but recall the trip to the lake two summers ago. When she waded into the water, schools of minnows would scatter from the treacherous upheaval caused by the shifting of sand under her feet. She now realized that, today, she became the sand between her toes that drove those minnows away.

If My Life Were Annotated

1.
I mark me up in a soft pink highlighter, barely noticeable,
         my time in running cars.
I flip me and draw a dash through flower-shop doorbells,
through *Crunch* bars, fun-size.

2.
Mine is a jagged yellow right through stories of my ex,
my high school years.
I uncap a ballpoint pen and annotate:
I'm still stuck in my head.
Then,
I am still stuck in my head, somewhere around my big toe.

3.
The pen is alien: I spend most of my time knifing in and
         out of excerpts of *Blue's Clues* and my family's fake
         Christmas tree, inserting branches in one by one.
There's a curious notation I can't make out on the years
         concerning my half-sister's conversion to
         Jehovah's Witness.

4.
I am riddled with coffee-rings and sticky notes.
I am giddy, ink-poisoned.
I am the stuff of dissertations.
Lines from my childhood to snow angels at age 22 traverse
         my back, laying waste the curvature of my spine.
I am drawing connections to Joyce, Milton, and Faulkner,
         comparing my escapades to Don Quixote, my
         resolve to that of Ahab – the tragedy of my life is
         covered in a number of Shakespeare's plays.

5.
I have never had the chance.

I never let myself alone in a room with a broad table and
        the appropriate lighting.
Afraid what I'll find with an arsenal of pens, highlighters,
        and white-out.
Marking up the years of my life and fracturing them to
        fragments I stitch to make a Frankenstein of me.

If Instructions Were Not Included

Inspiration is like a gun:
you need ammo, and the right kind.

Revise:
it's like a hammer
pound
now
pound
that nail will drive
eventually.

Revise:
backfire –
big noise, little substance.

You told me it doesn't fit in your pocket:
it isn't a gun, after all.

My mother used to clip letters from newspapers:
shook them like dice and tossed them in the air
and they fell like light from fireworks and I caught
them on my tongue like sulfur from an atom bomb
and now all I can say are words that begin with b's
and s's.

I used to skip rocks beyond the bay:
bang, bang, bang against the sea.

If We Were Connected

1. Day After
Janet flips the page of her newspaper
and starts mouthing words as she reads.
Kyle slurps up soggy frosted flakes
without taking his eyes off the Sports
section. Janet sighs, "Mother and child
killed in car blaze on I-91 yesterday."
She is reciting. Kyle says, "Hmmm,"
and dips below the surface pulling up
just milk this time. "Jeter hit a pair
of doubles." He dabs his chin
with a used napkin. "Asshole."

2. Eighteen Miles Out, Day Of
I see a deer just past the railing. She doesn't
seem nervous. Not like I always imagine
them being. This one is uprooting
daffodils a few feet from the highway. Cars
are gridlocked for miles. Far off I see smoke being
slanted against the sky like a just-falling domino.
Someone honks and the deer darts away
from the highway like a flicked marble.

3. Concussion
The mother awoke with one thought:
I need to fix that leaky faucet.
Water was beginning to pool
in the sink.
She could hear the timbre of the droplets
change as the puddle got bigger. Then –

why did she think of her brother-
in-law? A
carpenter with calloused thumbs
from years of quick inspections. He

once drove a nail
through his left thumb and kept
hammering because he couldn't
feel it. Maybe it
was the sound she heard close to her ear:

like a saw going through wood.
What was that? It must
be morning.
The sun was bright and felt a lot closer.

4. Cone Man
That's all I am. If it wasn't this stretch of highway
it would be another with the same damn mile
markers, an equally bad wreck, and a cattle
call of pissed off drivers pissed off at me where I drop
my cones. There was training for this job – fucking
riot if you ask me. Some corporate heads or something
that I never seen before or after since drive us down
to an empty parking lot. Start laying out cones like fixings
on a sandwich, moving 'em back and forth and telling
us this was the correct way and why that way
was dangerous and all this B-S about frontlines
of the *War on Secondary Automobile Accidents*.
What a crock! I put cones in the shape of a backslash
so some already dead shithead who probably
forgot to use her turn signal when changing lanes won't
cause another accident because other shitheads
wouldn't look up from their cell phones.
The only perk is pocketing the stuff that gets thrown
out in the crash. Not last week I found a perfect
working iPhone fifty feet away – not a scratch.
And this one I'm working now had some demons.
Found a nine-inch bowie knife not far away. Unsheathed.
Now tell me what kind of housewife carries
something like that. Freaks if you ask me.

5. The Man With the Knife
was the only one
who stopped.
Years ago his friend had told
him about a study:

how a person is more likely to be
assisted in an environment that
presents *less* potential rescuers
rather than *more*.

The man supposed
that this
is what was on his mind

when he decided
to stop. Then

he was perched on one knee, contorting
his back to get an angle
that allowed him to
hack
at the mother's

seatbelt. A crumpled-up accumulate like

a used tissue was this car
blocking one lane of
traffic. The man saw what could
have been unpackaged
steaks strapped

into what remained of
the passenger side backseat. He
heard gasoline

accumulate on the ground. A pounding

metronome.

More drops sought to
unfurl the pool
into a stream like a tongue;
taste buds throbbing for a well-

known source of combustion. The man
dug deeper into the belt, moved his
tongue around in his mouth. The knife sounded
like a saw

going through wood.

6. The Tennis Ball
Thwack.
Catch.
Thwack.
Catch.
For the millionth time against
the back of the headrest.
Late for dinner.
Thwack.
Sirens.
Thwack.
Feeling like
Thwack
a melting
Thwack
snowman.
Traffic.
Busted car on the shoulder.
Inching.
Thwack.
Car insurance.
Seatbelts?
Watered down soda.

Thwack.
Water.
Hose.
Thwack.
Late for dinner.

If the Wolf Hired an Attorney

I. Opening Statement

Ladies and gentlemen of the jury, this is a textbook case of slander. My client has done nothing more than live his life in a manner that takes full advantage of the rights and liberties promised to him by the United States Constitution. the very same rights that separate us from the Commies, The rights that you, your honor, preserve for the citizens of this fine country every day. My client is guilty of a lot of things: zeal, conviction, eccentricity. But not of being the heinous monster that a prejudiced court of public opinion has made of him.

II. The Three Little Pigs v. The Wolf

The claims brought to the court by this trio of swine: assault and damage to personal property. These pigs claim that my client went from "house" to "house," wreaking havoc, threatening their lives, and causing damage to the point where their structures were felled. Now if you notice, I put the word *house* in quotation marks because only someone with a healthy sense of humor could consider a pile of straw and sticks a house. My client was only attempting to point out the structural vulnerabilities of their...I'm sorry, I just can't refer to them as houses any longer. While his methods were, admittedly, unorthodox and extreme, I believe his point was made: a house that can be toppled by a strong exhale is not a house at all.

III. Little Red Riding Hood v. The Wolf

My client has been charged with invasion of privacy and assault by the young woman in the red hoodie. She claims that my client became infatuated with her, stalked her, arrived at her grandmother's before her, ate her grandmother, dressed in her grandmother's clothes, and attempted to seduce her. My client does not deny dressing in woman's clothing, but that is no crime. My client even admits to being in her grandmother's gown and in her grandmother's house, but the reason is far less devious than this lady would have you believe. My client had been engaged in a secretive relationship with this young woman's grandmother for over a year. Miss Red Riding Hood interrupted one of their role-playing games and found my client in her grandmother's clothes under her grandmother's sheets. She couldn't come to terms with what her grandmother was, so she spun this tale to demonize my client.

IV. The Wolf v. The Boy Who Cried Wolf

My client wishes to sue the adolescent who repeatedly cried his name and accused him of attacking a flock of sheep. On the night in question, when the boy sang out at the top of his lungs that he saw my client chasing sheep, my client and the boy were getting drunk on a hill just above the flock of sheep. Before you judge my client, understand that he was confused about the true age of the boy. The boy told my client that he was seven years old which, to my client, means that the boy was forty-nine – well past the legal drinking age. In the inebriated state, the boy suggested that the two of them play a little trick on the townspeople. He told my client to hide behind the bushes and to jump out once the townspeople showed up. My client agreed and proceeded to stumble behind the bushes where he passed out. Once the boy called out "Wolf!" the townspeople ran to him and saw that both the sheep were still there and there was no wolf. The boy laughed as a nervous reaction, so he tried it again minutes later and was met with the same result. Now the boy was mad and began furiously chucking empty beer bottles off the hill towards the sheep, cursing my client. The sheep scattered and the boy saw this as the perfect opportunity to exact his revenge on my client.

V. Closing Arguments

Ladies and gentleman of the jury, I believe I have made my case adequately. The charges my client is faced with today are mere fairy tale.

If You Could Melt Between City Cracks

You tell the worms what a sight it is up there, all
they're missing:
the combustible
cacophony of jazz bands seeping through closed night club
doors,
lights so bright night is just daytime with a burnt crust,
a world void of soil and roots – everything
they wanted to hear.

You didn't tell them about fishhooks or Styrofoam cups,
the whir of a schooner's engine,
or seagulls not stuffed on cotton candy. You never told
them about the concept of bait,
the carrot and the stick, that they were the ones destined to
be dangling from
a thin nylon string for all the fish told about the open bars
above sea level.

If You Even Smoked Nowadays

Hesitating for a moment with your poem
over a fireplace you said you'd replace years ago,
you think, *It won't burn for long*
but at least then, it's something.

You're about to toss it before the brilliance
that unburdened you those hours of ink
blots and suddenly important housework
strikes. Tripping over poorly placed

area rugs, you rush to your sock
drawer and pull out your stash.
Just a few pinches, licks away from
floundering similes and a mediocre

understanding of meter. You place
the poem flat on the table and smooth it out.
I shouldn't do this, thinking of all the letters,
exclamation points you'd be inhaling. *I'll*

need to get my hands on some carp, as your poem
connected growth and maturity to swimming
upstream. Not your finest work. *I don't even*
like fish, but you knew you'd eat it. Your only

fear is what would eat you. Knowing you used
the word "gnash," you only thought it fitting
that it would be the one, tongue protruding,
salivating from the open curve of 'g,'

gripping gleaming kitchenware, leading
personified extension cords and tree limbs
(your metaphor for mankind's exploitation
of nature) shouting, "I will not make a liar

out of Merriam-Webster!" So you decided
against it, the words salvageable,
but already found your poem burning
to its end in your ashtray.

If The Wind Changes or Dead Leaf Poem

The leaf said,
Don't come any closer! I'll do it!

The other leaves swayed.

That's it!

He was not meant for this world
or maybe the world was not ready
to find meaning in him.
Whatever the case,
he jumped.

It was a graceful plunge,
the leaf police would later
report to his leaf wife,
filled with many ascents
and crescent-shaped falls.

A lovely eulogy was interrupted
by his alcoholic leaf cousin
when he vomited on the casket
meant for symbolic purposes –
the casket, not the vomit;
his body was never recovered.

He was described as a fun-loving
leaf, who liked strong gusts
of wind in the summer –
he liked the feeling of it through his stem.
How could this have happened?

Soon a cult was formed.
They praised this leaf as a visionary,
the only one who got it,

who knew this earthly
body was a tomb,
a straight jacket,
which must be cast off
and thrown to the wind.

It wasn't long until
he gained a following –
eager young minds ready
to be liberated like their prophet.

A mass suicide was plotted.
The pigs tried to shut it down,
but the leaf chief was a believer,
so it was to no avail.

One by one they shook
free from their branches
and glided to be crushed
under the sneakers
of high school dropouts.

They called it Fall.

If The Moon Monologues

Un-ink your quills, writers. Stop
trying to romanticize the 'moonlight.'
There is no such thing.
Your intelligence misleads you to believing
there are rungs on this ladder of the
cosmos. Dust is all you are. Rock
is all I am. Stop painting faces
on soulless things.

If I Misplace Bones

5p.m. – 10p.m. Dish Washer
We manufacture lakes
to submerge discarded metals
with crust and uneaten food
caked desperately
for fear of abandoning
sinking ships.
These waters holding more promise
than what's written
on your yellowed parking tickets:
the letters F-I-N-E a mantra
forgotten
when all you want is to see her face,
to name every knuckle in her hand,
bend them so you can see
them pushed closer to the surface
where there is air.
White not being a color in the pallete
but the canvas,
and her bones.
Push harder.
Stack them high.
There's that tower we built,
a rotted staircase.
Say, "skip the seventh step,"
if anyone asks.
"It's made of shipwrecks,"
what we had handy,
but now it creaks and wakes
the neighbors.
If anyone asks,
say you know nothing of towers,
shipwreck, or air.
Say you've never seen her before
if anyone asks.

10:30p.m. – 6:45a.m. Warehouse Employee
A ringing
from a gunshot
I don't remember
hearing.

.22, I think.

Cardboard hearts
self-proclaimed self-
preservationists proclaiming:

Do not cut with knife.
Tear open here.

But I only ever seal
them or watch them
sealing – I'm a bleeding
heart, I suppose.

In a different context
I find the word
"seal" a homonym
used in much the same
way as "Fire!"
running towards
the catastrophe,
pulling plastic,
correcting lids,

putting lids on situations.

There are subtle differences.

If In Need of a Mirror

Take sand – this is not a metaphor
for time – and mix it with hose water

in a glass jar your father used to keep
nails in. Cut a single sheet of computer

paper in five equal parts (if needed,
use a ruler – inches count) and write

five secrets in hurried ballpoint pen
on each scrap. Don't think, this is important,

the most important things rise first.
You lied about how long it took you

to brush your teeth. You turned without
signaling. You never forgave your cousin,

not really. You've never read Paradise Lost.
You took an apple from a basket. Now fold

each sheet three times, or crumple
them all into one ball. It's either/or,

there is no middle ground. Stick you secrets
in the jar and let them sit until they sink

to the bottom. Time may vary for this step,
so don't hold your breath. Leave the jar

somewhere you can't reach it, and if you
remember to check on it again, it's already

too late.

If You Leave The Radio On

"Since U Been Gone"
has been stuck in my head all day and I can't
stop yelling the chorus in my car, humming
inaudibly on sidewalks, free associating the lyrics
with missing children press conferences - I need
help. I listen to progressive metal, bands that
would slay Kelly Clarkson and offer her body
as tribute to The Dark Lord (or at least that's
what everyone thinks they would do) and here
I am fist pumping my way down I-91
for shuttle buses to pass by filled with all my metalhead
friends (who apparently got a group rate or something)
to peer in and shake their heads disapprovingly
when they see that my hand is, indeed, in a full
fist and that I am not extending my index
and pinky in the air to signify that the music to
which I am listening would cause the greatest
ruckus possible. This is all your fault. All the love
you have given me, all the happiness you have
brought me apparently made me soft. That time
you cupped my face in your hands when I was
hysterical and told me to 'man up,' the exact
words I needed to hear, must have been
poison to my ears because when I swooned
- and men can swoon too, dammit - I must
have acquired a taste for that fluffy, cutesy,
habit-forming drivel of pop music that I have
always abhorred. It doesn't matter that that
music reminds me of the time we drove
down to the Cape on a scorcher with the windows
down (because, apparently you cannot
stand the taste of the artificial cool of the
air conditioner) blaring music against

the endless whirr of highway tires. I love you,
and I don't care what tumors I have to grow
to grow old with you.

If Stanley Kubrick Wrote a Children's Book

1. Conception
He'd title it:
A Horse Named Stuffed.
"A lesson of loss taught
through the most immediate
and intimate forms
of disembowelment
and taxidermy."

2. Fruition
Vivid depiction of the taxidermist
cartooned, hand hovering over a tray
of glass eyes

Turn the Page

The horse,
mid-autopsy abandoned haphazardly
at a time where crudely drawn forceps
were stuck in and now stick up out
of the abdomen

Turn the Page

A black and white photograph
of a man, brow furrowed, tongue
out, concentrating, aiming a 12-gauge
shotgun down at a lying horse

Turn the Page

Whistling taxidermist,
needle and thread, working.

3. Reaping
The kids would grow up to be lawyers
and doctors, some municipal workers,
but all monitored after years and sobering
years of "How could we expose them to that filth?"
passed. Parents would tattoo "Damaged Goods"
to their children's foreheads and read at rallies
from their own essays titled "Eulogy for My Child's
Innocence."

Then ex-hippies cured by neckties
and coffee mugs would construct
soapboxes out of the first amendment
and free speech and shout through
man-sized megaphones about the purity
of art, the danger of fascism, and the sanctity
of a child's choice to choose when
and by what means they're allowed to see
a female's breasts in the media.

Others would catch the highlights of the debate
- out of context – during commercials for grenade-
slicing knives and a plastic do-dad that could
hang a semi-truck from a ceiling fan.

4. Retrospect
All would wonder if their blinders
were on tight enough.

If This Poem Were Rejected

Dear [Prospective Contributor],

We regret to inform you that your insult to every decent aspect of art that you call your poetry submission did not make it through the first pass of readings. In fact, under my bidding, a committee has been formed to determine why anyone would consider this writing fit to be read by another human being. However, we do thank you for considering our magazine as a resource for publishing your horrific writing. We wish you luck in your future writing and publication efforts, but we see little to no promise in you and hope you actually take this as an embargo treaty of sorts and spare other editors a drunken night standing at the edge of a five-story ledge by refusing to ever submit your work anywhere again.

Sincerely.

ABOUT THE AUTHOR

David G. Walker's first poems were published in 2014: just after the ink was drying on his MFA from Southern Connecticut State University. Since that time, he has published work sporadically with high points and dry spells abounding. His previous two chapbooks – *Pause: A Collection of Moment Poems* and *Donating Organs in Boxes* – were published by *Finishing Line Press*. In 2016, his poem "California" won the Steel Pen Conference Creative Writing Contest and his poem "Cathedral" was nominated for Best New Poets in 2018. Currently, he lives in Massachusetts with his wonderful wife, Caitlin; his two children, Mikey and Ellie; and his cat, Eva.

www.ingramcontent.com/pod-product-compliance
Lightning Source LLC
Chambersburg PA
CBHW020956030426
42339CB00005B/128